£14.95

BRISTOL TO TAUNTON

including Weston-super-Mare

Vic Mitchell and Keith Smith

MP Middleton Press

Cover picture: No. 6000 **King George V** *approaches Weston-super-Mare with a down train and is about to obscure the gasworks siding. The train on the left is leaving Locking Road station on 20th September 1958. The locomotive still carries the bell today; it was attached for a tour of the USA in 1927. (N.L.Browne)*

Published April 2003

ISBN 1 904474 03 9

© *Middleton Press, 2003*

Design   Deborah Esher
*   David Pede*
Typesetting   Barbara Mitchell

Published by
*   Middleton Press*
*   Easebourne Lane*
*   Midhurst, West Sussex*
*   GU29 9AZ*
Tel: 01730 813169
Fax: 01730 812601
Email: enquiries@middletonpress.fsnet.co.uk

Printed & bound by Biddles Ltd,
*   Guildford and Kings Lynn*

CONTENTS

ACKNOWLEDGEMENTS

We are very grateful for the help received from many of the photographers and also from P.G.Barnes, W.R.Burton, L. Crosier, G.Croughton, N.Langridge, R.A.Lumber, C.Maggs MBE, Mr D. & Dr S.Salter, R.E.Toop, E.Wilmshurst, E.Youldon and our very supportive wives, Barbara Mitchell and Janet Smith.

I. 1947 Route map (Railway Clearing House)

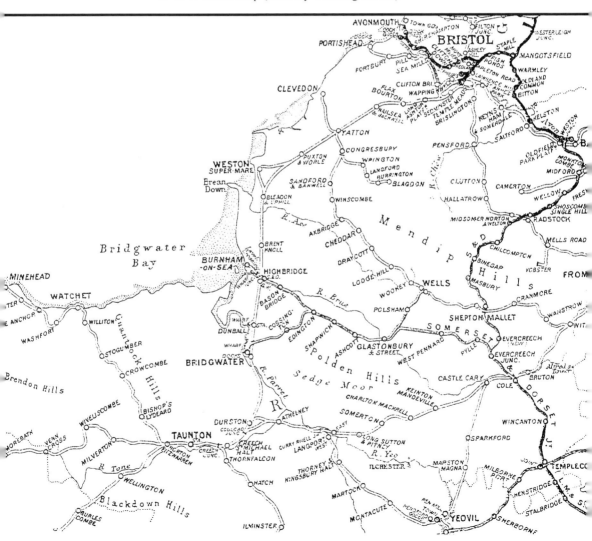

GEOGRAPHICAL SETTING

Before the railway era, Bristol was a well established inland port and trading centre, noted for non-ferrous metal production and having many collieries nearby. Surrounded by Limestone hills, the city's main line to the west climbs onto one such ridge in its first five miles. On its descent it passes the site of a long-closed colliery near Nailsea.

Most of the remainder of the route is on fairly level Marl, although for about five miles either side of Highbridge it traverses Middle Lias Limestone, also fairly level. Weston-super-Mare developed as a resort on a west-facing bay situated between two impressive Limestone headlands.

South of this town, the route passes through a cutting at Bleadon & Uphill, which was made in the Limestone forming the western extremity of the Mendips. The River Axe is crossed in this vicinity, the other waterways of note being the River Yeo near Yatton, the River Brue at Highbridge and the River Parrett at Bridgwater, the railway wharf on this being to the north at Dunball.

The route is in Somerset, except in the Bristol area, its county town being reached at Taunton. This is bisected by the River Tone, which is a tributary of the Parrett.

The maps are at the scale of 25ins to 1 mile, and north is at the top, unless otherwise indicated.

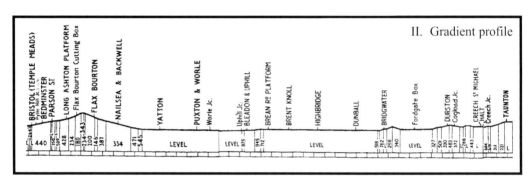

II. Gradient profile

HISTORICAL BACKGROUND

The Great Western Railway opened between Bath and Bristol in 1840 and trains from London began running on 30th June 1841. The Bristol & Exeter Railway had the same broad gauge of 7ft 0¼ ins and the same engineer, I.K.Brunel. It opened from its own terminus in Bristol to Bridgwater on 14th June 1841 and was extended to Taunton on 1st July 1842. Trains reached Exeter in 1844 and the BER became part of the GWR in 1876.

Weston-super-Mare was served by a single line branch from the opening of the main line. The branch was doubled in 1866, converted to mixed gauge in 1875 and replaced by the present loop line on 1st March 1884.

The dates of other associated lines on the route are thus:

	Opened	Closed to passengers
Portishead	1867	1967
Clevedon	1847	1966
Cheddar	1869	1963
Burnham	1858	1951
Glastonbury	1854	1966
Yeovil	1853	1964
Chard	1866	1962

The GWR was nationalised in 1948 to become the Western Region of British Railways. Changes initiated in the mid-1990s resulted in services on the route being provided by 2000 by First Great Western, Virgin CrossCountry and Wales & Borders.

PASSENGER SERVICES

In this section we consider down trains running on at least five days each week. The 1842 service terminating at Bridgwater comprised eight weekday and five Sunday trains. By 1850, the figures were nine and three, these changing little in the subsequent 30 years.

Departures from Bristol in July 1882 provide an interesting example, the number of stops on the route being in brackets.

am
4.15	Taunton	(4)	*
7.10	Taunton	(12)	
8.10	Weston	(7)	
10.5	Weston	(3)	
10.49	Weston	(7)	
11.5	Taunton	(9)	

pm
12.10	Taunton	(0)	*
12.35	Taunton	(6)	*
12.55	Taunton	(12)	*
1.45	Weston	(7)	
2.26	Taunton	(0)	*
3.0	Weston	(7)	
3.25	Taunton	(9)	*
4.40	Yatton	(3)	
5.15	Weston	(1)	
5.41	Taunton	(0)	*
6.0	Weston	(1)	
6.15	Taunton	(12)	*
8.15	Taunton	(2)	* S
9.0	Weston	(7)	

* continues west
S slip coach for Weston

On Sundays, there was one non-stop and two calling at all stations with connections at Weston Junction to and from the town.

The example below is from June 1961 and lists stopping trains only. At that time, they all ran via Weston-super-Mare.

am
6.47	Taunton
7.20	Weston
7.45	Taunton
8.20	Weston
9.0	Taunton
10.45	Weston
11.53	Weston

pm
1.0	Yatton
4.20	Taunton
4.45	Weston
5.15	Taunton
5.20	Yatton
5.32	Weston
6.10	Weston
6.33	Weston
7.45	Taunton
9.43	Weston

There were eleven fast trains during the day on the full length of the route, with a further 13 terminating at Weston-super-Mare.

By way of comparison, the 2003 timetable showed 37 through trains on weekdays, with 18 on Sundays and about eight terminating at Weston daily. The destination options throughout the ages have been diverse and many are included in the photograph captions.

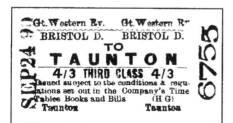

This timetable features overnight trains running from the North-east to the South-west along the route for the benefit of holidaymakers in the Summer of 1950.

TABLE 30 **THROUGH TRAIN SERVICES**
NEWCASTLE, YORK, BRADFORD, SHEFFIELD, AND WEST OF ENGLAND, Via Gloucester and Bristol

WEEK DAYS ONLY

Column notes (top table), left to right:
- *Friday nights only and will not run after 14th September — Through Train Newcastle to Penzance — Buffet Car Newcastle to York (arrive 6 0 a.m.)*
- *Friday nights only 20th July to 17th August inclusive only — Through Carriages Newcastle to Newquay (arrive 6 0 a.m.)*
- *Friday nights only and will not run after 14th September — Through Train Sheffield to Newquay (arrive 6 0 a.m.)*
- *Friday nights only and runs 29th June to 31st August inclusive only — Through Train Leicester to Torquay and Paignton*
- *Through Train Nottingham to Torquay and Paignton*
- *Friday nights only and will not run after 7th September — Through Train Sheffield to Torquay and Paignton*
- *Friday nights only — Through Train Bradford to Torquay and Paignton*

Station	p.m.	p.m.	p.m.	p.m.	p.m.	p.m.
NEWCASTLE ... dep.	4A 0	...	...	...	...	...
Durham	4 22	...	...	...	...	...
Darlington	4 53	...	...	...	...	...
YORK	5 45	...	...	...	...	...
BRADFORD (Forster Square) dep.	...	...	...	...	...	8 50
Leeds (City)	...	...	...	...	...	9 20
SHEFFIELD (Midland)	7F10	7A18	...	10 50	10A20	10 40
Derby (Midland)	8F 5	8A22	...	9A55	11 23	11 50
Nottingham (Midland) dep.	...	...	9B12	...	...	...
Leicester (London Road)	...	...	10D10	...	...	...
BIRMINGHAM (New Street) dep.	9 11	a.m.	a.m.	a.m.	a.m.	1S 5 (a.m.)
Worcester (Shrub Hill)	8a44	...	...	...	...	...
Cheltenham Spa (Lansdown)	10 15	10 25	12S39	1S16	1S35	...
Gloucester (L.M.R.)	10 31	10 41	...	...	...	...
BRISTOL (Temple Meads) arr.	11 26	11 36	1S34	2S11	2S47	3S30
BRISTOL (Temple Meads) dep.	11 40	12 0	1S45	2S20	3S 0	3S50
Weston-super-Mare ... arr.	a.m.	...	...	...	...	...
Bridgwater General	...	...	...	...	...	...
Taunton	12S40	1S 0	2S39	3S20	4S10	4S50
EXETER (St. David's)	1S25	1S46	3S29	4S 5	4S55	5S40
Dawlish	...	...	4S 7	...	...	6S 5
Teignmouth	...	...	4S20	4S35	5S30	6S15
Newton Abbot	1S59	2S19	...	4S46	...	6S25
Torre ... arr.	...	...	...	5S10	5S49	...
TORQUAY	...	...	4S40	5S15	5S52	6S52
Paignton	...	...	4S50	5S24	6S 0	7S 5
Kingswear	...	...	...	...	...	...
PLYMOUTH (North Road) ... arr.	3S15	3S25	...	...	...	...
PENZANCE	6S15	...	...	...	...	...

Column notes (bottom table), left to right:
- *Friday nights only and will not run after 24th August — Through Train Newcastle to Torquay and Paignton*
- *will not run after 8th September — Through Train Birmingham (New Street) to Weston-super-Mare*
- *Saturdays only — Through Train Walsall to Torquay, Paignton and Kingswear*

Station	p.m.		a.m.	a.m.
NEWCASTLE ... dep.	9A 5	...	...	...
Durham	9 29	...	...	...
Darlington	10A 2	...	...	...
YORK	10 55	...	...	...
BRADFORD (Forster Square) dep.	...	...	...	...
Leeds (City)	...	...	...	...
SHEFFIELD (Midland)	12S25 (a.m.)	...	...	...
Derby (Midland)	1S30	...	...	...
Nottingham (Midland) dep.	...	...	...	...
Leicester (London Road)	...	...	...	...
BIRMINGHAM (New Street) dep.	a.m.	...	6A50	7 30
Worcester (Shrub Hill)	...	...	...	7a30
Cheltenham Spa (Lansdown)	3S39	...	8 7	8 42
Gloucester (L.M.R.)	3S58	...	8 35	9 0
BRISTOL (Temple Meads) arr.	4S53	...	9 47	9 56
BRISTOL (Temple Meads) dep.	5S 0	...	9 50	10 5
Weston-super-Mare ... arr.	...	...	10L25	...
Bridgwater General	...	...	...	...
Taunton	5S58	...	...	11 14
EXETER (St. David's)	6S45	...	...	12 7
Dawlish	7S18	...	...	...
Teignmouth	7S30	...	...	12 35
Newton Abbot	7S43	...	...	12 45
Torre ... arr.	8S 3	...	...	1 8
TORQUAY	8S 7	...	...	1 11
Paignton	8S16	...	...	1 20
Kingswear	...	...	...	1 41
PLYMOUTH (North Road) ... arr.	...	...	...	...
PENZANCE	...	...	...	...

A—Seats can be reserved in advance on payment of a fee of 1s. 0d. per seat (see page 28)

B—Applies on 22nd June and 7th and 14th Sept. only. Through carriages from Nottingham on these dates only. Seats can be reserved in advance on payment of a fee of 1s. 0d. per seat (see page 28)

D—Seats can be reserved in advance on payment of a fee of 1s. 0d. per seat except for Fridays 22nd June and 7th and 14th September (see page 28)

F—Seats can be reserved in advance on payment of a fee of 1s. 0d. per seat for Fridays 20th July to 17th August inclusive only (see page 28)

L—Locking Road Station (Weston-super-Mare).

S—Saturday mornings

a—Change at Cheltenham Spa (Lansdown)

¶—From 20th July to 17th August inclusive these carriages are detached at and leave Sheffield at 7 18 p.m. (see next column)

The June 1955 summary timetable shows some trains scheduled to use Locking Road station. Their times are marked L.

Table 15

LONDON AND BATH SPA, BRISTOL AND WESTON-SUPER-MARE

WEEK DAYS

		E R		S R	Q R		E R	S R	E R	S R M R		S M R		E R	S R
	am	am		am	am		am	am	am	am		am		pm	pm
PADDINGTON .. .. ..dep	5 30	7 30		7 30	8A45		9A 5	9A 5	9A15	9A15 11A15		11A15		1 15	1 15
Bath Spa...arr	8 12	9 52		10 2			11 10	11 16	11 50	11 50 1 1		1 1		2 52	3 1
Bristol (Temple Meads).. .. ,,	8 34	10 13		10 26	10 30		11 30	11 40	12 11	12 12 1 22		1 24		3 15	3 23
Weston-super-Mare General.. ,,	9h46			11 30	11 22		12 20	12L21	1 17	1 16 1 56		2 -6		4 5	4 15

WEEK DAYS—continued

			E R	S R		R			R	E R	E		S	F	
	pm	pm	pm	pm		pm	pm		pm	pm	pm		pm	pm	pm
PADDINGTON .. .. ..dep	1 18	2 35	4A15	4A15		5A 5	5 14		6A30	7A50	9A50		9A50	11 35	11 50
Bath Spa...arr	4 3	5g29	6 24	6 42		6 54	8 11		8 25	9 41	12*38		12*32	1*55	2D36
Bristol (Temple Meads).. .. ,,	4 32	5g52	6 45	7 5		7 15	8 31		8 50	10 4	1* 3		1* 0	2*21	3D 3
Weston-super-Mare General.. ,,	5 25	6g48	7 24	7 41		7 57	9 21		9 42	11 5					3D42

SUNDAYS

		R		R		R	R							
	am	am		am		pm	pm	pm		pm	pm	pm		pm
PADDINGTON .. .. ..dep	9 5	9J55		11A15		12 30	1A20	4 15		5 30	7A15	7 30	9A50 11 40	11 50
Bath Spa...arr	11 52			1 30		3 20		6 57		8 0	9 26	10 22	12*38 2*10	2*36
Bristol (Temple Meads).. .. ,,	12 15	1 18		1 56		3 40	5k 8	7 20		8 23	9 49	10 43	1* 3 2*35	3* 3
Weston-super-Mare General.. ,,	1 6	2 0		2 30		4 26	6k10	8 25		9 21		11 56		3*42

WEEK DAYS

						R		R		E R	S	R		Z R	S R	E R
	am		am		am		am		am		am	am	am		am	am	am
Weston-super-Mare General..dep			12B15		3 55		7 0		8 20		8 45	8 45	10E54		10 40	11A 5	11 15
Bristol (Temple Meads)...... ,,							7 45		9 0		9 35	11A45			12 0	12 0
Bath Spa... .. .. ,,	12B 3		12B35		4 25		8 5		9 18		9 53	9 55			11 50	12 20	12 20
PADDINGTON...........arr	2B55		3B25		7 25		10 0		11 8		12 20	12 35	1 45		2 25	2 35	2 30

WEEK DAYS—continued

	E R		S R	S R		S R	E R		Q R	E R		E R M R	S M R			
	pm		pm	pm		pm	pm		pm	pm		pm	pm		pm	pm
Weston-super-Mare General..dep	12 41		12 57	1T58		2 15	2 15		3 3	3 3		4A35	4A40		5 40	6 50
Bristol (Temple Meads)...... ,,	1A50		1A50	2 35		2 57	3 0		4A30			5A27	5A27		6 20	7 35
Bath Spa... .. .. ,,	2 8		2 10	2 56		3 18	3 20			4 34		5 49	5 49		6 45	7 57
PADDINGTON...........arr	4 0		4 30	5 25		5 40	5 35		6 15	6 43		8 0	8 0		9H20	10 50

SUNDAYS

				R				R			R			
	am	am		am		pm		pm	pm		pm	pm		pm	pm
Weston-super-Mare General..dep	12N15	8 5		11 33		12 44		4 19	4 45		5 55	6 45		9 22	9 50
Bristol (Temple Meads)...... ,,	3 55	9 5		12 28		1 35		5 15	5 30		6 50	7 25		11637	12*15
Bath Spa... .. .. ,,	4 25	9 27		12 50		1 55		5 35	5 52		7 10	7 47		12* 3	12*35
PADDINGTON...........arr	7 25	12 20		3 55		4 30		7 55	8 40		9 35	10 30		2*55	3*25

A Seats can be reserved in advance on payment of a fee of 1s. 0d. per seat (see page 26)
B Monday mornings only
D On Sundays arrive Bath Spa 2 33 am, Bristol 3 0 am, and Weston-super-Mare 3 41 am
E Except Saturdays
F Runs Friday nights until 2nd September inclusive only
G Bristol (Stapleton Road)
g Via Devizes

ll On Saturdays 5 minutes later
h On Saturdays arrive 9 17 am
J Change at Swindon. See also Note "A"
k Via Badminton (change at Swindon)
L Locking Road Station
M The Merchant Venturer
N Third class only for a portion of the journey
Q The Bristolian (Limited accommodation)

R Refreshment Car provided in some cases for a portion of the journey only
S Saturdays only
T Locking Road Station. See also Note "A"
Z Saturdays only and runs 16th July to 3rd September inclusive only
* am

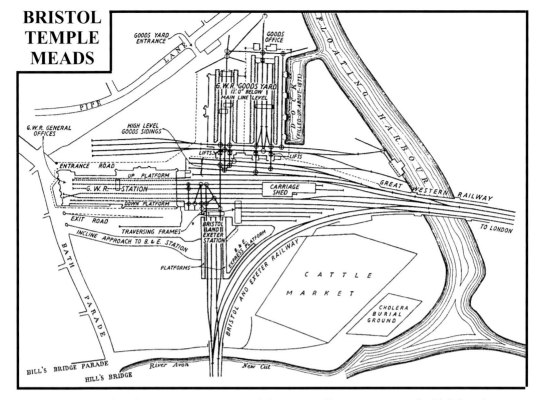

BRISTOL TEMPLE MEADS

III.   The 1845 plan shows two separate termini connected by curves, one of which has the name "B&E Express Platform". This was used by about three London trains each day and soon proved inadequate as traffic increased. The GWR station was built in the parish of Temple, on a field known as Temple Meads, and was used by BER trains initially. Reversals ceased in 1845 when that company's own terminus came into use. The GWR terminus was also used by Midland Railway trains from Gloucester until a new joint station was erected on the curve in 1873-78. It originally had three through platforms. (Railway Gazette)

1.   The island platform was brought into use in January 1899 and there were subsequently six platform faces and four through lines. The extra space had become available following the abandonment of the broad gauge in 1892. This view of the fine curving shed is from 1906. (British Railways)

IV. The 1918 survey includes the 1874 goods depot, which was accessed differently from that shown on the 1845 plan and thus did not have wagon hoists. The offices near the bottom of the map were those of the BER and they still stand today (picture 6). The sidings top right are those of the Midland Railway. The passenger entrance near the cattle market was lost when extra platforms were built in 1933-35. This map continues at the top of the next one.

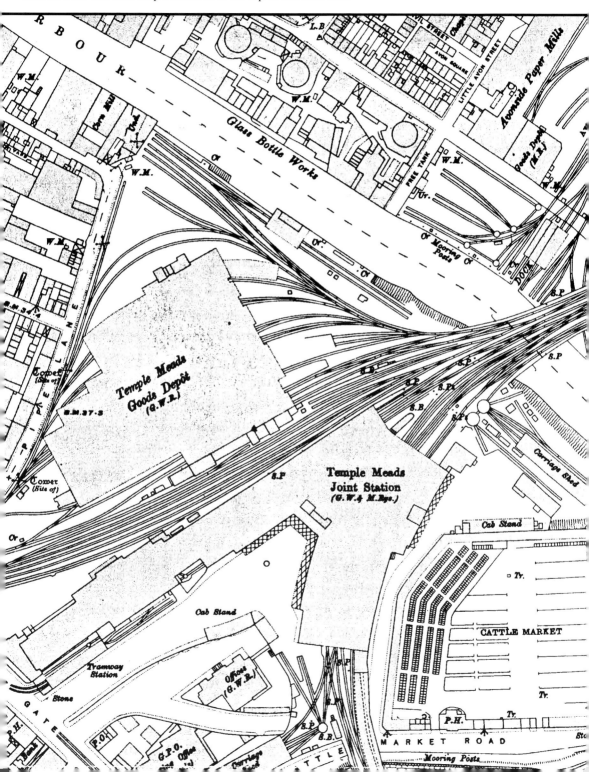

2.   This northward view is from 1934, when further major platform alterations had just been completed. Nos 1 to 4 had been added on the right and no. 11 on the left. Those in the original GWR building became 12 to 15. The locomotive leaving platform 4 is running onto the "Engine Line", which continues into the distance and southwards to the engine shed. (Brunel University/Clinker coll.)

3.   Recorded on 26th August 1956 was 4300 class 2-6-0 no. 6391 at platform 9, while no. 5094 *Tretower Castle* runs through non-stop. Colour light signalling came into use on 24th November 1935. (R.M.Casserley)

4.   The south end of the station is seen on the same day. No. 5971 *Merevale Hall* stands at platform 4, while the rear of its train is at no. 3. On the right are nos 1 and 2, which were used for local trains. (H.C.Casserley)

5.   Class 47 no. 1601 runs through with oil from Avonmouth to Exeter City Basin on 1st March 1973, while coal empties run north. The platforms on the left were used mainly for mail traffic at this time. (D.H.Mitchell)

6.   The entrance is below the gothic-style tower. The main train shed from the 1870s fills the centre of this 1977 view. On the right is the BER office block, the rear of which appears in pictures 2 and 5. (F.Hornby)

7.   A class 119 DMU arrives from Taunton having passed under Bath Road bridge from which pictures 2 and 5 were taken. This bowstring structure dates from the 1933 alterations and is seen in the 1980s. (M.Turvey)

8.   Steam rises from the leading Mk. I coach as no. 45076 waits to leave platform 6 with the 16.08 (Sundays only) Derby to Newton Abbot service. A new signalling panel came into use on 9th March 1970, when the platforms were renumbered again. No. 6 became 3 and 4 (1 and 2 were bays) and 13 was relegated to parcels, only to be reinstated in 2001. (G.Gillham)

9.   The bridge at the London end contained a mailbag conveyor linked to the letter sorting office. DMU no. 150280 is at platform 11 on 10th November 1993, while the twin-axle cars of no. 143603 stand at the disused no. 13. There was no track at no. 14, but this was replaced in 2001 and the platform numbered 15 for passenger use. The south end of the track at no. 13 now has buffers. (M.Turvey)

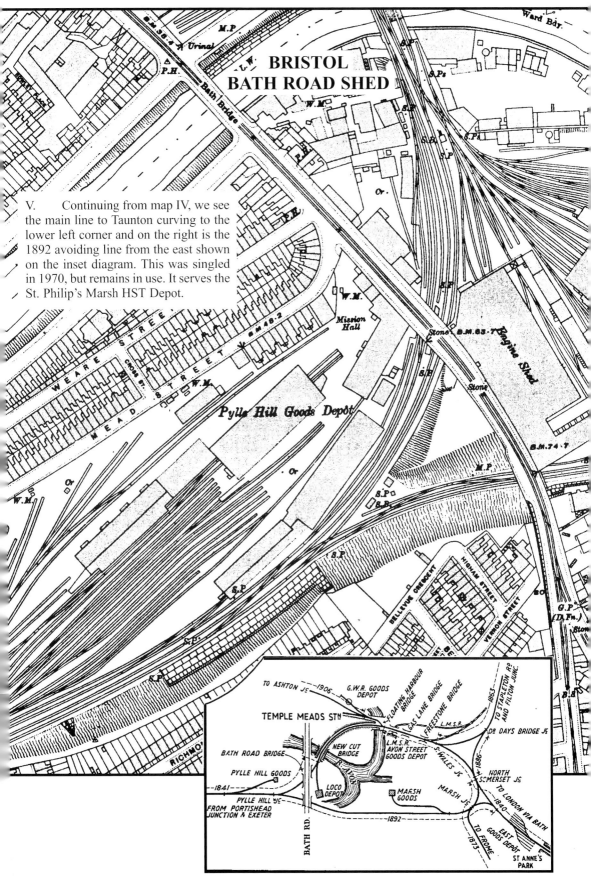

**BRISTOL
BATH ROAD SHED**

V. Continuing from map IV, we see the main line to Taunton curving to the lower left corner and on the right is the 1892 avoiding line from the east shown on the inset diagram. This was singled in 1970, but remains in use. It serves the St. Philip's Marsh HST Depot.

Pylle Hill Goods Depot

10.   A panorama from platform 4 in July 1935 includes no. 3407 *Madras* and 2-8-0 no. 4701. The BER built its engine shed on this site and the GWR used it from 1876. It was rebuilt to the form seen in 1934. (R.S.Carpenter coll.)

————————▶

11.   The forge was recorded on 29th April 1950, while "Dean Goods" no. 2445 was under repair. The shed (coded 82A) closed to steam traction on 11th September 1960. There were 90 locomotives allocated here in January 1938 and 91 in February 1954. (H.C.Casserley)

————————▶

12.   The diesel depot used most of the old buildings and is seen on 1st May 1982, as no. 45130 leaves to join a train in the station. There are 12 roads under cover, but the depot closed on 24th July 1995. (M.Turvey)

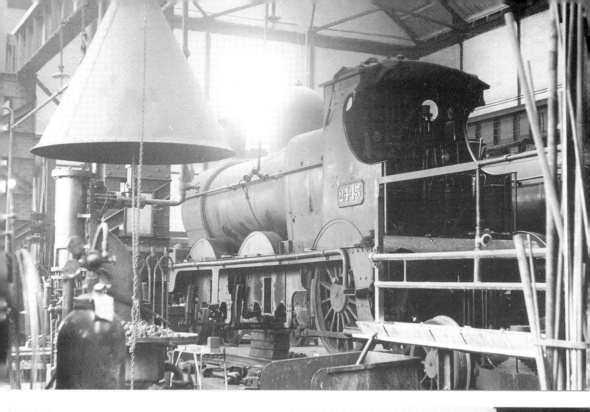

SOUTH OF BRISTOL

13.   A westward panorama from Bath Road on 1st March 1973 includes class 45 no. 30 with "The Devonian", the 10.50 from Paignton to Leeds. On the left is the single track from Marsh Junction and on the right is the once-hectic Pylle Hill goods depot in terminal decline. (D.H.Mitchell)

14.   Further south, we witness no. 47033 running north with empty coal hoppers on 13th October 1981, while a string of DMUs pass through the 1967 washing plant. The number of running lines in this vicinity had been increased to six in 1933, but has been four since 1970. The goods depot sidings converge on the right. The washer was not used after 2000. (G.Gillham)

Gt Western Ry   Gt Western Ry
H.M. FORCES ON LEAVE
Parson Street   Parson Street
TO
BRISTOL (T.M.)
THIRD CLASS
Bristol (T.M.)   Bristol (T.M.)
FOR CONDITIONS SEE BACK   W.D

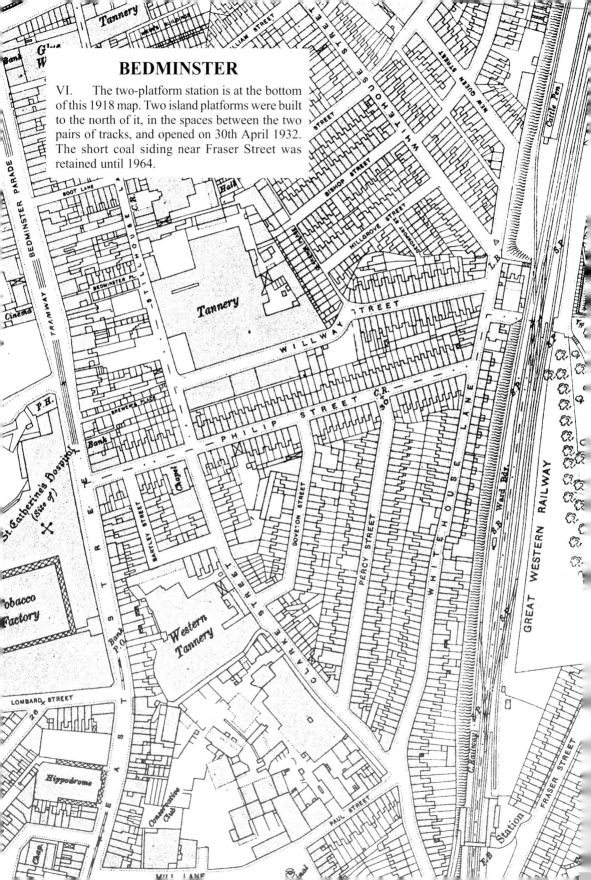

BEDMINSTER

VI.   The two-platform station is at the bottom of this 1918 map. Two island platforms were built to the north of it, in the spaces between the two pairs of tracks, and opened on 30th April 1932. The short coal siding near Fraser Street was retained until 1964.

15.   This is a northward view of the pre-1933 station, as depicted on a postcard. It had opened on 27th May 1884 and was extended in 1908. There had earlier been a ticket platform and an excursion platform in this vicinity. (Lens of Sutton coll.)

16.   The 1932 station is seen in July 1956, looking towards Bristol. The signal box is at the commencement of the six-track section and its 74-lever frame was in use from April 1932 to April 1970. Platforms 1 and 4 are no longer in use. Staffing ceased in September 1968; there had been 15 men here in 1938. (R.M.Casserley)

SOUTH OF BEDMINSTER

17.   The seven Malago Vale carriage sidings were in use from 1932 until 1988. There was a colliery siding beyond the footbridge from 1879 until about 1915. The signal box had 81 levers and lasted from 1932 to 1970. (P.J.Garland/R.S.Carpenter coll.)

VII. Track designations from 1934 to 1970.

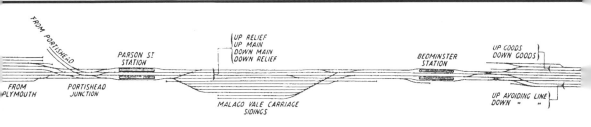

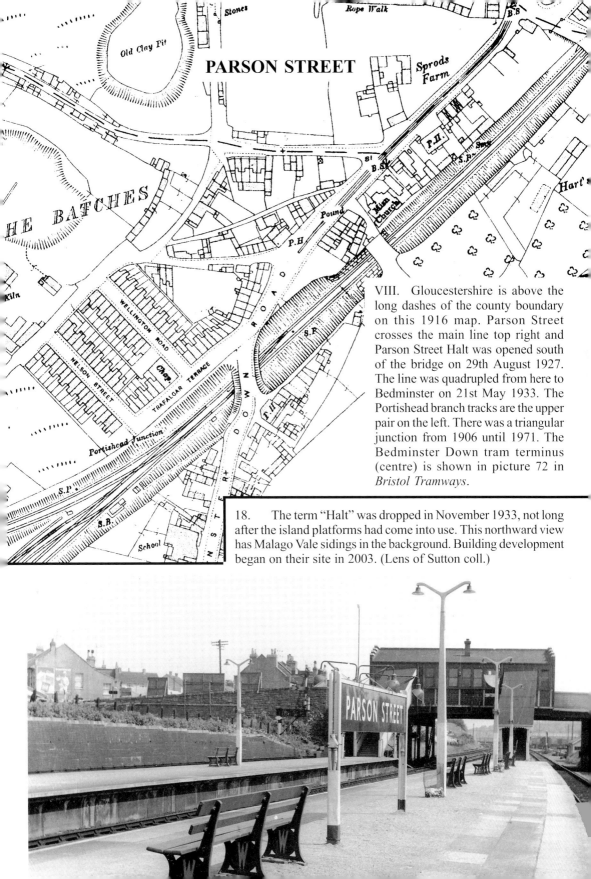

PARSON STREET

VIII. Gloucestershire is above the long dashes of the county boundary on this 1916 map. Parson Street crosses the main line top right and Parson Street Halt was opened south of the bridge on 29th August 1927. The line was quadrupled from here to Bedminster on 21st May 1933. The Portishead branch tracks are the upper pair on the left. There was a triangular junction from 1906 until 1971. The Bedminster Down tram terminus (centre) is shown in picture 72 in *Bristol Tramways*.

18.   The term "Halt" was dropped in November 1933, not long after the island platforms had come into use. This northward view has Malago Vale sidings in the background. Building development began on their site in 2003. (Lens of Sutton coll.)

19.   No. 5096 *Bridgwater Castle* approaches with a Taunton-Bristol stopping train in about 1955. The lines to Portishead curve right beyond the 1933 bridge. Parson Street Junction signal box was to the left of the third coach. It functioned from 13th November 1932 until 6th December 1971 and had 82 levers. (R.S.Carpenter)

20.   A northward view from the same bridge includes the street level station and evidence of the great scale of the civil engineering work undertaken to fit four tracks and a station in the space provided for two broad gauge lines. The short tunnel was eliminated. This picture is from March 1965. (P.J.Garland/R.S.Carpenter coll.)

21.　　Looking from the other side of the bridge we see no. 3764 leaving West Depot Up Yard in March 1960, with the Portishead branch on the right. Lost in the mist are the eleven sidings of West Depot Down Carriage Yard. They closed in 1971. (H.Cowan)

22.　　The "Bristol Harbour Special" ran to Wapping Wharf several times on 28th September 1985 behind ex-BR 2-6-0 no. 46443 as part of the GW150 celebrations. The Portishead branch had been closed to freight in 1981 and was reinstated in December 2001 to serve the Royal Portbury Dock. On the left is the little used 1975 Bristol Freightliner Terminal, which has subsequently closed. Further west, there had been a siding for South Liberty Colliery in the 1870s and for a brickworks later. (S.P.Derek)

LONG ASHTON

IX.   Opened as Long Ashton Platform on 12th July 1926, the suffix was dropped on 23rd September 1929. It is noted as HALT on the 1946 edition at 1 ins to 1 mile, although not shown as such in GWR timetables. The triangular junction for the Portishead branch is also shown, as is the location of the next station, Flax Bourton.

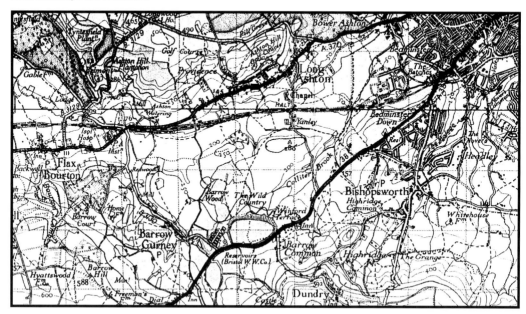

23.   Most photographers have avoided this location and so we can only offer this indifferent view of no. 13197 with an up LMS excursion. The halt ceased to appear in timetables after 24th September 1950. Tickets issued dropped from 4267 in 1930 to 1466 in 1938. (C.G.Maggs coll.)

FLAX BOURTON

24.   The first station was known as "Bourton" until 1888 and was closer to the tunnel than its successor. Its west portal is behind the station master in this record of a broad gauge 4-2-2 passing under the bridge, which was provided to carry a public footpath and an aqueduct. (LGRP/NRM)

25.   An up train was photographed at the same location, this giving us the opportunity of examining the complexity of mixed gauge track. The third rail had been laid in 1875. The swinging lantern door was contrary to the rule book. There was a staff of eight in the early 20th century. (LGRP/NRM)

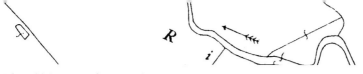

X.   The 1931 survey features the second station, which opened on 2nd March 1893 and, unlike its predecessor, was provided with a siding. Although the population was only 201 in 1901, much traffic had arisen due to the development of the nearby Tyntesfield Park, by an entrepreneur who had made a fortune importing Peruvian bird droppings, guano. The crane could lift 3 tons. The up refuge siding became a loop in 1958.

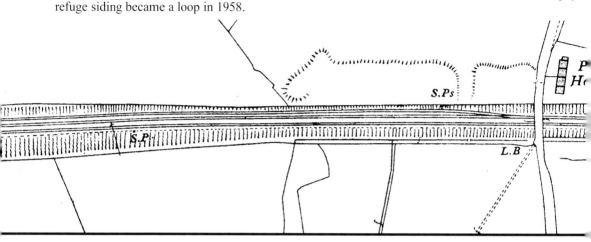

26.   The second signal box was close to the signals (left) and was in use from 1893 to 1958. The right signal gave access to the up loop until 1971. No. 5098 *Clifford Castle* speeds passed the small goods yard, which closed on 1st July 1964. The station building was still standing at the end of that century, albeit disused. (M.J.Stretton coll.)

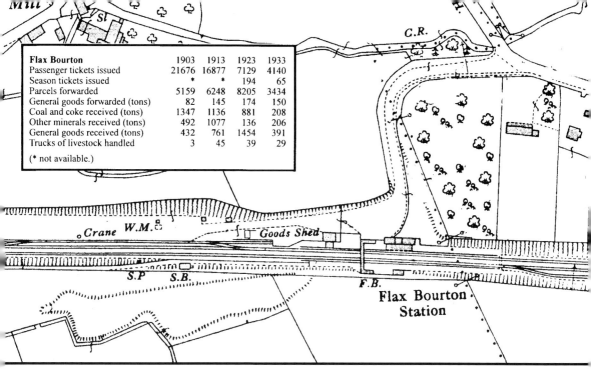

Flax Bourton	1903	1913	1923	1933
Passenger tickets issued	21676	16877	7129	4140
Season tickets issued	*	*	194	65
Parcels forwarded	5159	6248	8205	3434
General goods forwarded (tons)	82	145	174	150
Coal and coke received (tons)	1347	1136	881	208
Other minerals received (tons)	492	1077	136	206
General goods received (tons)	432	761	1454	391
Trucks of livestock handled	3	45	39	29

(* not available.)

27.　　Passenger traffic here ceased on 2nd December 1963, but the spacious 45-lever signal box remained in use until 6th December 1971. No. 4944 *Middleton Hall* is passing it and the multitude of point rods. Government fuel sidings ran from the loop/siding from 1958 until 1981 and were known as Tyntesfield Sidings. (M.J.Stretton coll.)

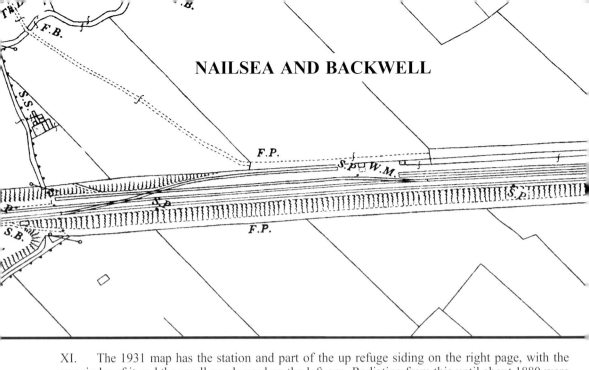

NAILSEA AND BACKWELL

XI.   The 1931 map has the station and part of the up refuge siding on the right page, with the remainder of it and the small goods yard on the left one. Radiating from this until about 1880 were private sidings serving Young Wood Colliery and Nailsea Colliery. A tramway continued from the former to Whiteoak Colliery.

28.   The station opened with the line and is still in use today, albeit with simple bus shelters. This 1949 view includes the 18-lever signal box, which was in use until December 1971. It was named "Nailsea East" until 1952, when "West" closed. Both are shown on the map as "S.B". (LGRP/NRM)

Nailsea and Backwell	1903	1913	1923	1933
Passenger tickets issued	25020	31358	27325	21249
Season tickets issued	*	*	1001	695
Parcels forwarded	2753	6472	5200	6193
General goods forwarded (tons)	163	235	632	727
Coal and coke received (tons)	4265	3469	5029	3383
Other minerals received (tons)	736	363	855	88
General goods received (tons)	429	1143	1286	792
Trucks of livestock handled	-	-	-	-

(* not available.)

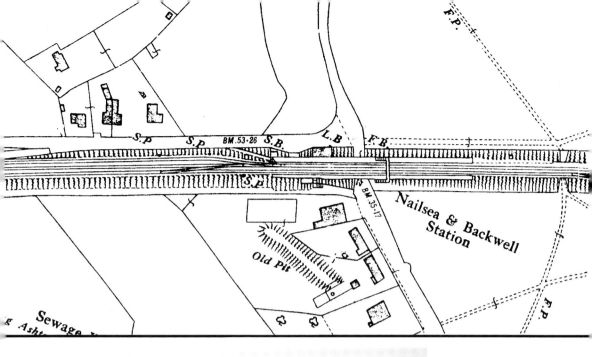

29. Two photos from 1962 complete our survey. This includes the up refuge siding; the down one is behind us. The goods yard is in the far distance; this closed on 1st July 1964.
(P.J.Garland/
R.S.Carpenter coll.)

30. Staffing ceased in September 1968. There had been eight men employed here in the 1930s. The suffix "Backwell" was used from 1905 to 1974 and again from 1977. The combined population of the two places rose from 2654 in 1901 to 7358 in 1961.
(P.J.Garland/
R.S.Carpenter coll.)

YATTON

XII.   The 1931 edition has the cabinet works of Wake & Dean Ltd top right, this having a private siding from 1919 to 1956. The Clevedon branch is on the left and the line to Cheddar is at the bottom. Lower left is the tiny gasworks. The engine shed closed in August 1960. The crane was rated at six tons in 1938.

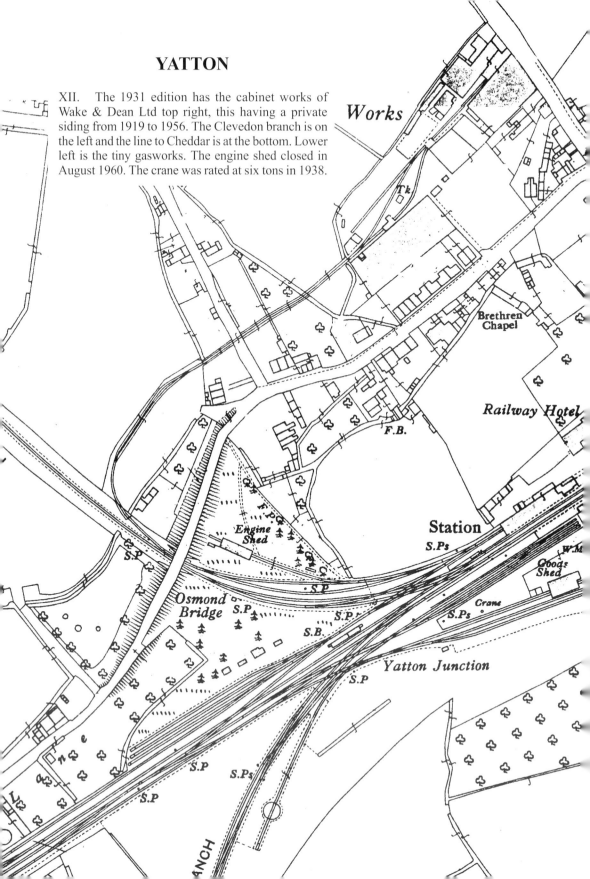

Works

Tk

Brethren
Chapel

Railway Hotel

F.B.

Station

S.Ps

W.M

Good
Shed

Engine
Shed

S.P

S.P

Osmond
Bridge

S.P

S.P

Crane

S.Ps

S.B.

S.P.

Yatton Junction

S.P

S.P

S.Ps

S.P

S.P

ANCH

31.   The station opened with the line and was named "Clevedon Road" until 1847, when the branch to that town opened. The staff level rose from 33 in 1903 to 40 in 1929.
(Lens of Sutton coll.)

Yatton	1903	1913	1923	1933
Passenger tickets issued	55958	57177	59898	62245
Season tickets issued	*	*	1001	606
Parcels forwarded	31168	34974	29952	11430
General goods forwarded (tons)	1468	1611	882	751
Coal and coke received (tons)	2367	2353	2784	1473
Other minerals received (tons)	1501	1034	643	224
General goods received (tons)	1781	2125	2416	4156
Trucks of livestock handled	246	220	313	106

(* not available.)

32.   A local stopping train runs into the down platform in about 1949, hauled by 2-6-2T no. 4142. There was quadruple track in the distance from 1925-1964, these dates applying also to East Box, which is represented by a white spot under the bridge. It had a 25-lever frame.
(J.H.Moss/R.S.Carpenter coll.)

33.   An up stopping train stands at the platform on 3rd July 1955 with one of the successful "Prairie" 2-6-2Ts, no. 5535. The Clevedon junction is to the rear of the train; the branch closed to passengers on 3rd October 1966. (F.Hornby)

34.   No. 4970 *Sketty Hall* departs for Bristol in March 1959 and passes the branch junction speed limit sign. A sheep market had been held to the right of the house. (H.Cowan)

Other pictures of this station are numbered 101 to 110 in *Branch Line to Cheddar*.

35.   A return excursion from Paignton to Nottingham approaches Yatton West box in August 1961. This had 129 functional levers and was in use from 1901 to 1962. The Cheddar Valley lines curve to the left, the branch closing in 1964. The goods yard closed on 29th November 1965. (R.S.Carpenter)

36.   Introduced in the area around 1960, DMUs still had to carry oil lamps when photographed on 16th April 1965. This example is working a stopping train from Taunton to Bristol and is passing under the roofless footbridge. (C.L.Caddy)

37.   Working the 17.22 Bristol Temple Meads service to Taunton on 12th September 1986 was no. 33062. By that time, cars were parked on the site of both branch bay platforms. The canopy came from Dauntsey and can be seen in pictures 19 and 20 in *Swindon to Bristol*. (D.H.Mitchell)

38.   A train of clay slurry tankers from Cornwall approaches on 26th July 2002, hauled by no. 66018. The building from Brunel's era had survived, moreover the ticket office was still in use. In the distance are the 1925 up and down loops; both were upgraded for use by passenger trains in October 2001. (M.Turvey)

39.   Huish Crossing box was built in 1925 and was probably the third on the site. It was photographed in 1965 and was closed in December 1973, when full lifting barriers came into use. The frame had 30 levers. (C.L.Caddy)

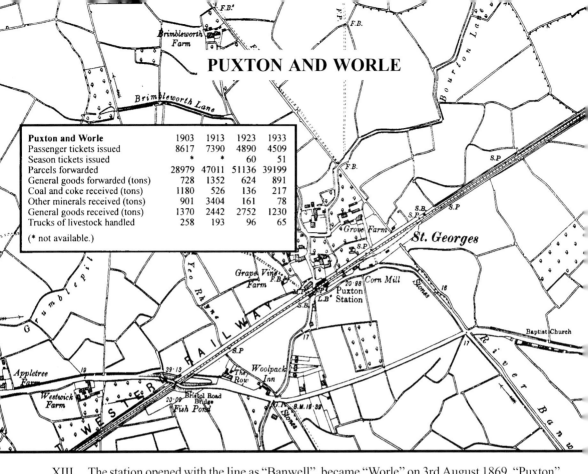

PUXTON AND WORLE

Puxton and Worle	1903	1913	1923	1933
Passenger tickets issued	8617	7390	4890	4509
Season tickets issued	*	*	60	51
Parcels forwarded	28979	47011	51136	39199
General goods forwarded (tons)	728	1352	624	891
Coal and coke received (tons)	1180	526	136	217
Other minerals received (tons)	901	3404	161	78
General goods received (tons)	1370	2442	2752	1230
Trucks of livestock handled	258	193	96	65

(* not available.)

XIII.   The station opened with the line as "Banwell", became "Worle" on 3rd August 1869, "Puxton" on 1st March 1884 and "Puxton & Worle" on 1st March 1922. This 6ins to 1 mile map is from 1932, although the name was not updated. It shows the goods shed, but not the second goods siding.

40.   Most of the goods yard is obscured by the porter, but part of the six-ton crane is evident. The staff rose from seven in 1903 to 16 in 1938 whilst traffic diminished, but so did working hours. (LGRP/NRM)

41.   Goods traffic ended on 10th June 1963, passenger trains ceased to call after 6th April 1964 and the photograph was taken one year later. This westward view includes the 23-lever signal box which functioned until 1972 when it became a crossing box. It was still in use in 2003. Beyond the crossing, on the up side, there was a siding for the London Co-operative Society from 1935 to 1966. (C.L.Caddy)

WORLE

42.   A new station was opened about half a mile west of the original one, on 1st October 1990. A class 143 unit is working from Bristol to Weston-super-Mare on 26th June 2002. (M.Turvey)

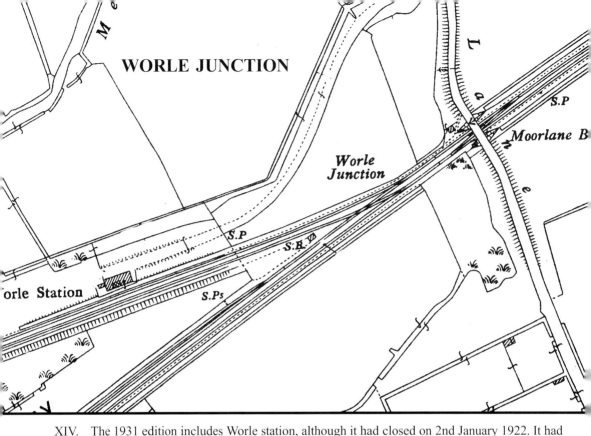

WORLE JUNCTION

Worle Junction

S.P

S.B.

orle Station

S.Ps

Moorlane B

S.P

XIV.   The 1931 edition includes Worle station, although it had closed on 2nd January 1922. It had opened with the direct line to Weston-super-Mare on 1st March 1884.

43.   Worle station and its approach road are on the right of this 1934 view, which includes the up refuge siding which was in use from 1885 until about 1964. (LGRP/NRM)

44.   This is a closer look at the disused Worle station in 1934. This route never received broad gauge track. (LGRP/NRM)

45.   This photograph is from the same viewpoint as no. 43 and shows that the Weston line had been singled. This took place on 31st January 1972, when the 20-lever signal box was closed. The HST is working the 14.20 Paignton to Newcastle on 12th September 1986. (D.H.Mitchell)

WESTON MILTON

Weston Milton
Halt

XV.   The 1936 survey shows semi-detached housing in the vicinity of the halt, which opened on 3rd July 1933.

46.   Weston's gas holders are in the distance in this photograph from the BR totem sign era, one such sign being evident on the left lamp post. Tickets issued were 758 in 1934 and 2312 in 1937. (Lens of Sutton coll.)

47.   A view towards Bristol in April 1965 includes the inclined path on the left and steps on the right. Only the up platform remained in use after the line was singled in 1972. (C.L.Caddy)

EAST OF WESTON-SUPER-MARE

XVI.   The Weston-super-Mare & District Electric Supply Co. Ltd. had a siding for its power station from 1928. It was in place until 1959. The tramway ran from 13th May 1902 until 17th April 1937.

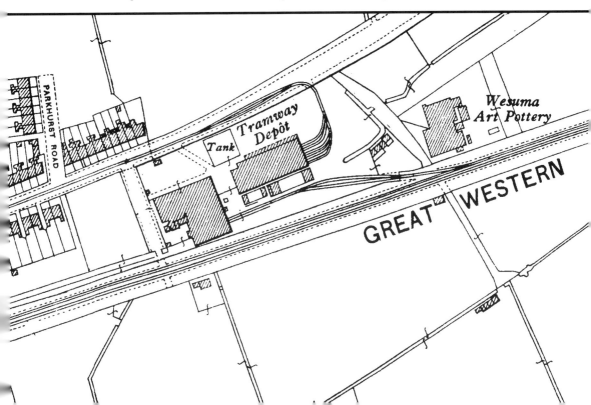

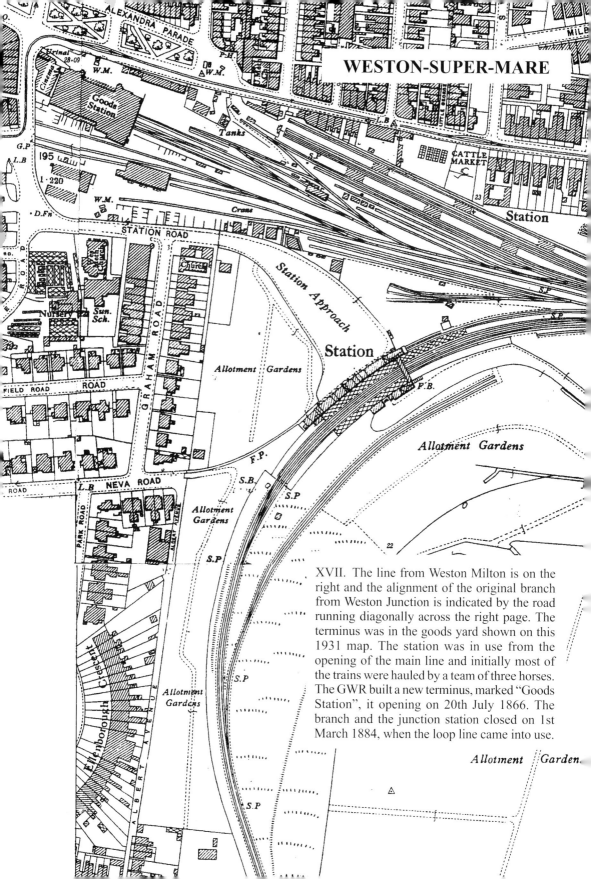

WESTON-SUPER-MARE

XVII. The line from Weston Milton is on the right and the alignment of the original branch from Weston Junction is indicated by the road running diagonally across the right page. The terminus was in the goods yard shown on this 1931 map. The station was in use from the opening of the main line and initially most of the trains were hauled by a team of three horses. The GWR built a new terminus, marked "Goods Station", it opening on 20th July 1866. The branch and the junction station closed on 1st March 1884, when the loop line came into use.

48.	A postcard view from the footbridge from above the down platform features trains in the up platform, up bay and loop. The latter lasted until 1970. The goods yard is obscured by the trains. (Lens of Sutton coll.)

49.	The 1884 station was lavishly appointed and constructed with a pleasing grey limestone. From 1903 to 1938 it had a staff of 55 to 62, with an additional 28 or 29 in the goods department. (Lens of Sutton coll.)

50.	The 1866 station was photographed in 1934, by which time it had been used exclusively for goods traffic for 50 years. (LGRP/NRM)

51.	Turning around on the same platform, we see that the other one was of great length as well. Other items of note are the stone-built engine shed and the six-ton crane. The roofs on the left are on the Locking Road platforms. (Lens of Sutton coll.)

52.   Locking Road station opened on 8th April 1914, its four platforms intended exclusively for excursion trains. They are on the right of this view from the end of the up platform in about 1948 - each one had three short canopies. (J.H.Moss/R.S.Carpenter coll.)

53.   Generous canopies were provided over the up platform and the bay. No. 5043 *Earl of Mount Edgcumbe* was one of the "Castle" class and is seen in about 1948. (J.H.Moss/R.S.Carpenter)

54.   A view towards the buffers at Locking Road shows four excursion trains having arrived in the rain on 14th April 1952. Note the old style of platform numbering. The name appeared in public timetables in the mid-1950s. (Lens of Sutton coll.)

55.   The imposing footbridge and stairway is seen from the down side in July 1955, with a large Austin and a small Morris in attendance. The station name had the suffix "General" from 21st September 1953 until 6th May 1958. (Lens of Sutton coll.)

56.   Wind breaks were thoughtfully placed on the platforms at this sometimes draughty place. Calling on 20th September 1958 is no. 6815 *Frilford Grange*. Up to 20 expresses would terminate at Weston on Summer Saturdays in the mid-1950s, with excursions adding to the traffic on Sundays. (N.L.Browne)

57.   Seldom photographed are the long fire irons and the ash pit hose that are required for engine disposal at the end of each working day. No. 4619 and no. 5950 *Wardley Hall* are also included, as is the exit from platforms 3 and 4 of Locking Road. (P.J.Kelley)

58.   The wagons on the left are standing on the line to the gasworks which carried fuel from 1883 until 1969. DMUs stand at Locking Road's platforms 1 and 2 as "Castle" class no. 5059 *Earl St. Aldwyn* leaves with the 8.0am Plymouth to Liverpool Lime Street on 18th June 1961. East Box was in use from April 1922 until January 1972, it having 113 levers in its frame. (M.J.Stretton coll.)

59.   A car park has been created on the site of Locking Road station which closed on 6th September 1964. The goods yard ceased to handle traffic on 20th June 1966, but some sidings remained in place until 1986 for the engineers. The 12.18 HST Weston-super-Mare to Paddington is leaving on 30th April 1982 and is about to pass two carriage sidings. Most of the area behind the train has since been used for a roundabout and car parks. (T.Heavyside)

60.   The main entrance was on the north side and is seen in 1985. Generous shelter was provided and ornamentation was limited to some dummy dormers and shapely chimney stacks. (C.L.Caddy)

61.   West Box had been behind the camera and its 21-lever frame was in use until 26th September 1955. Two photographs from 26th June 2002 show a station well conserved and cared for. Virgin CrossCountry offered such destinations as Dundee and Edinburgh. (M.Turvey)

62.   Local services were provided by Wessex Trains using mainly class 158 units, providing much improved comfort over the previous generation of DMUs. The lack of forward visibility and livery such as this were on their downside. The bay is used for engineering equipment. (M.Turvey)

2nd-SINGLE SINGLE-2nd

Puxton & Worle to

Puxton & Worle   Puxton & Worle
WestonMiltonHt   WestonMiltonHt
WESTON MILTON HALT

(W)   6d.   FARE   6d.   (W)

For conditions see over For conditions see over

621   621

2nd-SINGLE SINGLE-2nd

Nailsea & Backwell to

NAILSEA&B'WELL   NAILSEA&B'WELL
Flax Bourton   Flax Bourton
FLAX BOURTON

(W)   6d   Fare   6d   (W)

For conditions see over For conditions see over

049   049

SOUTH OF WESTON-SUPER-MARE

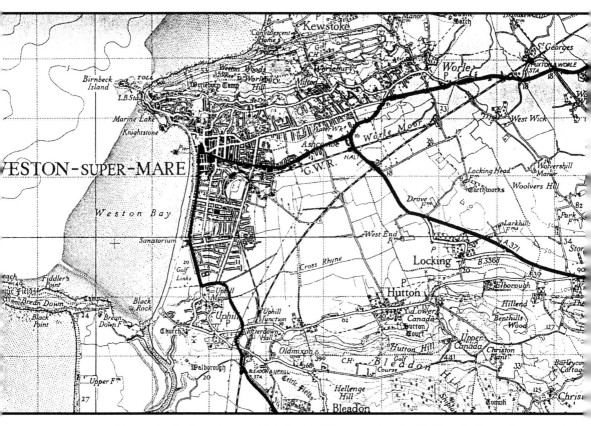

XVIII. Uphill Junction is the point at which the 1884 loop rejoins the 1841 main line. The route of the original branch is marked by a minor road on this 1946 map at 1ins to 1 mile. Hutton signal box was near the site of Weston Junction from 1940 to 1964 and it controlled access to the nine sidings of the Bristol Aeroplane Company.

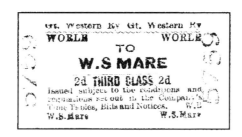

UPHILL JUNCTION

63.   A 1962 northward view includes the down refuge siding, which was available from about 1885 to 1972. An airport was created in the right background. (P.J.Garland/R.S.Carpenter coll.)

64.   The 14.25 Bristol Temple Meads to Taunton rejoins the main line on 12th September 1986 and will soon use the crossover in the foreground. The destination blind shows "Bristol" as part of the Passenger Deterrent Scheme that seemed to exist at that time. (D.H.Mitchell)

BLEADON AND UPHILL HALT

XIX. The 1936 survey includes a limestone quarry, which was served by a siding between about 1877 and 1918. The stone was apparently used for railway purposes. There is evidence of the earlier route of the A370.

65. No. 4905 *Barton Hall* approaches the station with a down goods train on 6th October 1962. The cutting is through the western extremity of the Mendips and the site of the quarry loading dock is evident on the right. (P.J.Garland/ R.S.Carpenter coll.)

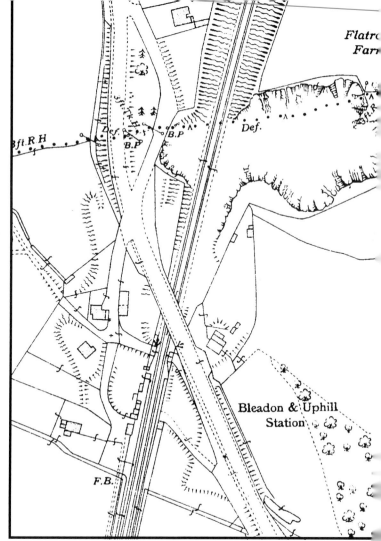

Flatro
Far

Bleadon & Uphill Station

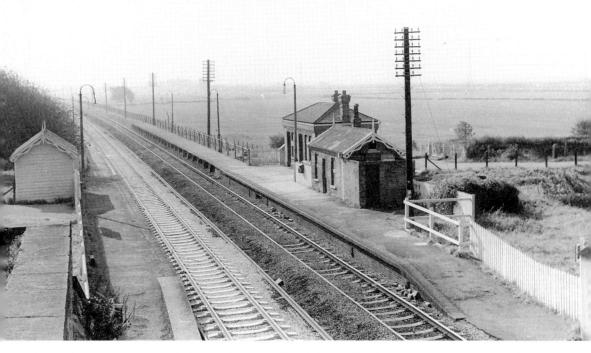

66. The station was recorded from the other side of the road bridge on the same day. There had been a signal box on the down platform until 1918 and there was a staff of five for most of the 1930s. (P.J.Garland/R.S.Carpenter coll.)

67. The bridge dates from road improvements around 1930, but an earlier abutment remains on the left. No. D7050 is speeding west on 29th August 1964. The combined population of the two villages was just over 1000 in 1901. (C.L.Caddy)

Bleadon and Uphill	1903	1913	1923	1933
Passenger tickets issued	9157	12482	6113	1726
Season tickets issued	*	*	45	31
Parcels forwarded	4980	10801	6330	1508
(* not available.)				

68.   Seen on the same day, the sign is in two parts as the station was simply "Uphill" until 1872. Staff were withdrawn in 1959 and the station closed on 5th October 1964. (C.L.Caddy)

69.   A private collector established the Somerset Transport Museum on the site and it was photographed in 1969. No. 1338 was built by Kitson in 1898 for the Cardiff Railway and became GWR property. It was moved from here to the Didcot Railway Centre. (T.Heavyside)

BREAN ROAD HALT

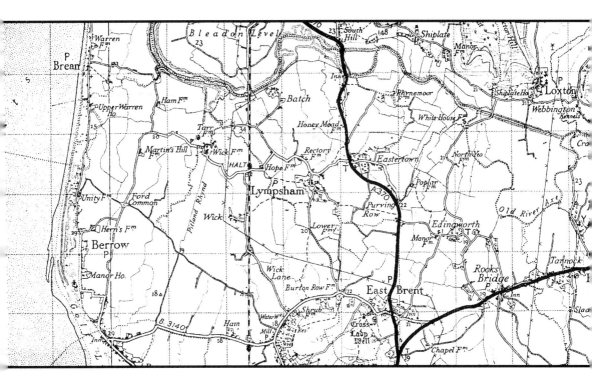

XX.   Brean is on the coast, almost two miles from its halt. Also shown on this 1946 map at 1ins to 1 mile is Brent Knoll station, near the lower border.

70.   A northward view from 1948 includes Lympsham signal box, which was open from 19th May 1921 until 21st December 1958. It had six levers and had formerly served at Cemetery Road, North Acton. (LGRP/NRM)

71.   Looking in the same direction about two years later, we join other admirers of the 2800 class of 2-8-0s. The halt was in use from 17th June 1929 until 2nd May 1955. (J.H.Moss./R.S.Carpenter coll.)

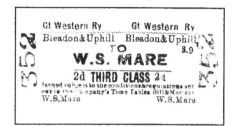

Gt Western Ry   Gt Western Ry
Bleadon&Uphill   Bleadon&Uphill
TO
W.S. MARE
2d THIRD CLASS 2d
Issued subject to the conditions&regulations set
out in the Company's Time Tables Bill&Notices
W.S.Mare   W.S.Mare

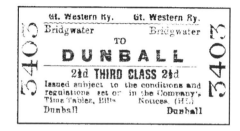

Gt. Western Ry.   Gt. Western Ry.
Bridgwater   Bridgwater
TO
DUNBALL
2½d THIRD CLASS 2½d
Issued subject to the conditions and
regulations set or in the Company's
Time Tables, Bills   Notices. (H.I)
Dunball   Dunball

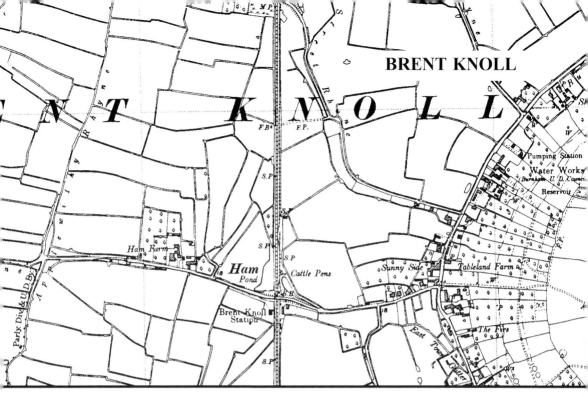

XXI.   The 1936 map at 6ins to 1 mile shows the relationship of the station to the community living on the road that curves around the foot of the 457ft. high Brent Knoll, an outcrop of limestone in this otherwise flat landscape.

72.   The straight track alignment is evident in this northward view from around 1960. The station opened in about 1875 and had a staff of 8 or 9 in the 1920s, when the local population was about 700. (Lens of Sutton coll.)

73.   The yard was north of the road bridge and closed on 10th June 1963. The signal box was to the right of the camera in this 1962 view. It had 26 levers and was in use until 31st January 1972. Camping coaches were allocated here in the Summers of 1938-39. (P.J.Garland/R.S.Carpenter coll.)

74.   The station ceased to be staffed after 5th October 1964 and was closed completely on 4th January 1971. No. D827 *Kelly* runs through on 29th August 1964 and is about to pass the unusual sign "3 GENTLEMEN". (C.L.Caddy)

HIGHBRIDGE

XXII. The 1930 edition has two stations near its lower edge, that of the Somerset & Dorset Joint Railway being on the right. This was incorporated into the Western Region of BR in 1948, but continued to be known as the S & D. Much of its route is shown on map I.

Tank

Bristol Bridge Brick Works

M.P

Kilns

S.B.

S.P

GRANGE AVENUE

Chy.

Kiln

Brick Works

Clay Pit

Goods Shed

Allotment Gardens

W.M

Cattle Pens

Walrow Terrace

GREAT WESTERN RAILWAY

Railway Hotel

S.B.

Cr

S.P

Cattle Pens

P.H

L.B

S.P

F.B.

Highbridge Junction

Station (G.W.R.)

S.P

Station (S. & D.J.R.)

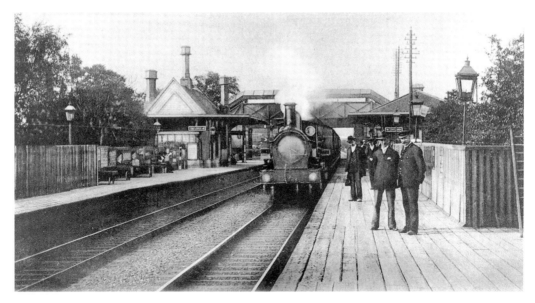

75.   This postcard view includes a train for the West and some of the staff which numbered 23 in 1903. This increased to 35 by 1933. (Lens of Sutton coll.)

76.   A 1928 official photograph helps to explain one reason why so much labour was required. Milk tankers ran direct from the creameries in later years. (R.S.Carpenter coll.)

77.   A northward view includes the goods yard and a perforated backing signal, which gave access to it and the line to the wharf. The box below it indicated which route was set. (LGRP/NRM)

78.   A closer look at the junction reveals the options. The line crossing was originally just a goods extension to the wharf from the Somerset Central Railway. This was initially worked by the BER, but it was extended to Burnham-on-Sea for passenger services in 1854 and later became part of the S & D. A six-ton crane stands beyond the dock. (J.H.Moss/R.S.Carpenter coll.)

79.   No. 4016 "Castle" class *The Somerset Light Infantry (Prince Albert's)* is on the crossing in about 1949 with a van train. West Box had 47 levers and served from about 1914 until 20th March 1972. It became "Highbridge Crossing" on 14th March 1965 when East Box closed. This is near the rear of the train and had an eleven lever frame. (J.H.Moss/R.S.Carpenter coll.)

80.   The exterior had become an architects nightmare with battens on the walls and two iron stovepipes protruding through an ugly lead roof. The name became "Highbridge West" on 5th May 1950 and "Highbridge & Burnham-on-Sea" on 30th June 1952, but reverted to plain "Highbridge" on 6th May 1974. However, "& Burnham" was logically restored on 13th May 1991. (J.H.Moss/R.S.Carpenter coll.)

81. The goods yard closed on 2nd November 1964, but a connection to the S & D route eastwards was retained until 1980. The complex shape of the footbridge was a legacy from the days when it extended to serve four other platforms. The 13.50 Weston-super-Mare to Taunton was recorded on 12th September 1986. (D.H.Mitchell)

The wharf, the S & D works and the other station are illustrated in pictures 10 to 37 in *Burnham to Evercreech Junction.*

82. No. 150234 is working to Bristol Temple Meads on 26th June 2002 and has just passed the goods loop, which can be used in either direction as two crossovers are provided. The train will have just passed the site of sidings laid down in 1940 at Huntspill for an Army depot. (M.Turvey)

DUNBALL

XXIII. The 1930 edition features Dunball Wharf, which was served by a tramway that was laid down by local coal merchants in 1844. It was acquired and improved by the BER in 1849 and much coal was imported from South Wales. It is shown connecting to an up goods loop, which at its north end served North End Cement Works. There was also a siding on the down side for Dunball Pottery, but further north. The two tracks pass over the A38 near the Greenhill Arms Hotel. There were no gates, a red flag being sufficient until closure on 22nd April 1967.

Inset is a United Molasses tanker on the wharf on 1st June 1966. (C.G.Maggs)

276
125

F.P.

F.B.

Railway Crescent

P.

Greenhill Arms
Hotel

Ps

W.M.

Dunball S

M.P.

M.P.

Tank

G.P.

ervoir Sl

M.P.

Dunball Clyce

M.P.

Stone

Highest Point to which
Ordinary Tides flow

M.P.

DUNBALL

M.P.

WHARF

M.P.

M.P.

P.O.

on

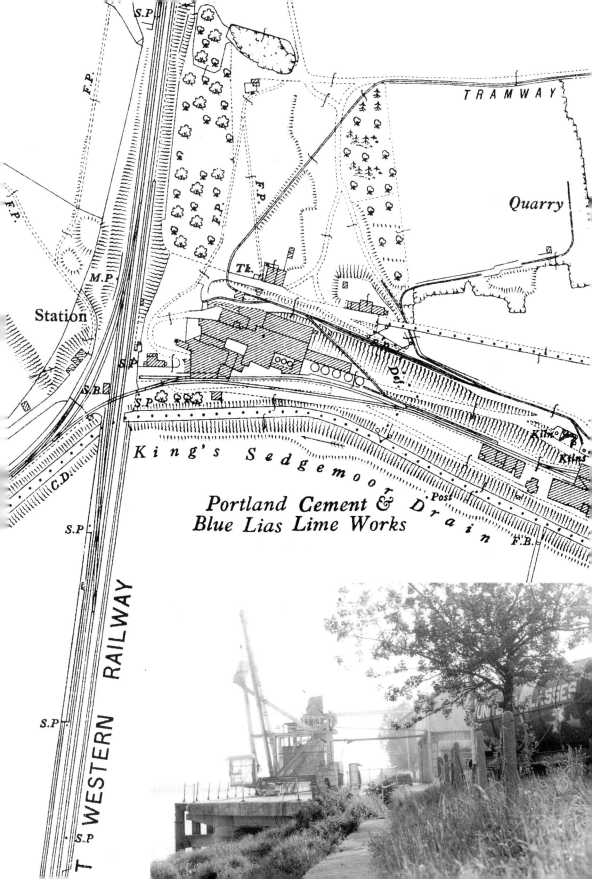

S.P.

F.P.

TRAMWAY

F.P.

F.P.

F.P.

Quarry

M.P.

Tk.

Station

S.P.

S.B.

S.P.

Del.

Kiln

Kilns

C.D.

S.P.

King's Sedgemoor Drain

Post

Portland Cement &
Blue Lias Lime Works

F.B.

S.P.

T WESTERN RAILWAY

S.P.

S.P.

←―――――

83. No. 72 *Exe* was of the "River" class and was photographed on the down line, opposite the signal box, in about 1905. The station probably opened in 1873 and is evident in the background. (R.S.Carpenter coll.)

85. Locomotives of the 1361 and 1366 classes worked the wharf lines, plus no. 1338 seen in picture 69. No. 1362 was recorded on 17th September 1958. An empty wagon was commonly used as a barrier next to one with a projecting load. (M.A.N.Johnston)

←―――――

84. A southward view in July 1958 has the up platform in the distance and a doubly fenced footpath to it across the bridge over King's Sedgemoor Drain. Access to the down platform was by a rough path over five tracks. The siding to the cement works had crossed the main line on the level, near the signal box, until the previous month - see map. (H.C.Casserley)

86.	Here is the path to the down platform in October 1962. The term "Halt" was applied on 6th November 1961 and closure followed on 5th October 1964. There had been a staff of four in the 1930s, but no public goods traffic was handled. Staffing ceased in November 1961. (P.J.Garland/R.S.Carpenter coll.)

87.	No. D7010 passes the point at which a siding once crossed on the level. The date is 6th October 1962. The 25-lever signal box and the connection in front of it ceased to be used on 11th July 1965. A ground frame was available at the north end of the loop until June 1967. (P.J.Garland /R.S.Carpenter coll.)

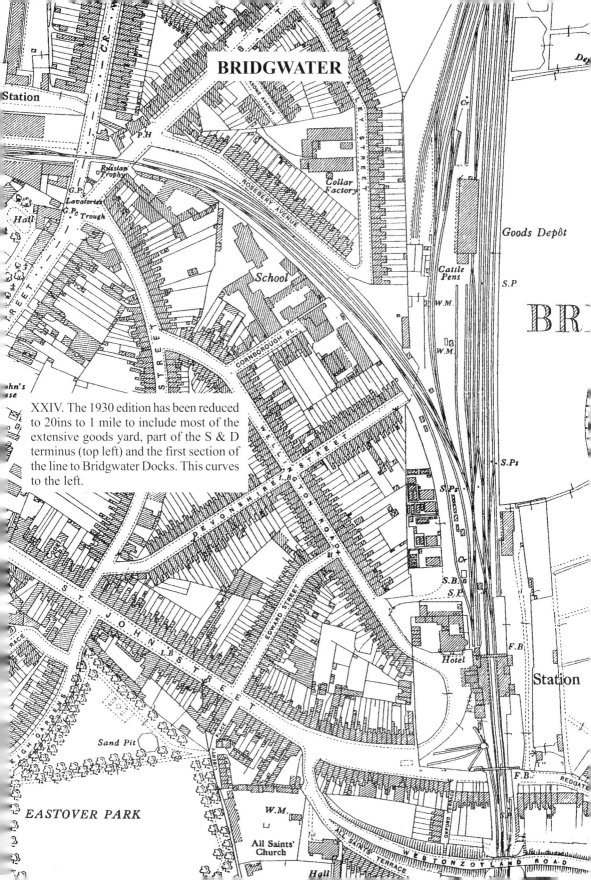

BRIDGWATER

XXIV. The 1930 edition has been reduced to 20ins to 1 mile to include most of the extensive goods yard, part of the S & D terminus (top left) and the first section of the line to Bridgwater Docks. This curves to the left.

Station

P.H

Russian Trophy

G.P.

Lavatories

G.P. Trough

Hall

Collar Factory

ROSEBERY AVENUE

School

Goods Depôt

Cattle Pens

S.P

W.M.

W.M.

BR

CORNBOROUGH PL.

WELLINGTON STREET

WELLINGTON ROAD

DEVONSHIRE STREET

S.Ps

Cr

S.Ps

S.B.

S.P

STREET

ohn's se

ST JOHN L.B. STREET

EDWARD STREET

Hotel

F.B.

Station

GHORE LANE

Sand Pit

LIBERTY STREET

OXFORD TERRACE

F.B.

REDGATE

EASTOVER PARK

W.M.

All Saints' Church

ALL SAINTS' TERRACE

WESTONZOYLAND ROAD

Hall

Cr

88.   A 1934 panorama includes the iron-clad parcels office (left), with its lantern roof, unusual on a building using mundane material. There was a staff of 32 that year, with a further 43 employed in the goods department. (LGRP/NRM)

89.   The impressive west facade was photographed in 1947, by which time it was shabby like most of Britain still recovering from the war. The suffix "Central" was applied from 26th September 1949 until 1st December 1952, when the S & D branch closed. (LGRP/NRM)

90.   No. 6829 *Burmington Grange* runs into the down platform with "The Devonian" on 17th September 1958. It went from Bradford to Paignton and called here at 4.54pm. There was a through train from Manchester and one from Liverpool at this period. (N.L.Browne)

91.   Working in the busy yard on 17th September 1958 were nos. 5571 and 1668. North of the station were sidings for British Cellophane Ltd and the cattle market. (N.L.Browne)

92.   Passing the wartime "Pill Box" on 6th October 1962 was a "Warship" class diesel with an up express. Beyond the bridge on the right were sidings serving eight different firms, but most ceased to be used by the end of that year. There was a level crossing here in broad gauge days. (P.J.Garland /R.S.Carpenter coll.)

93.   The yard was still busy on 12th September 1986. No. 47130 is reversing the 13.50 Speedlink departure to Severn Tunnel Junction on the line that once ran to the docks. Artificial fertiliser is an important traffic here. (D.H.Mitchell)

94.   The gantry seen in the previous photograph was provided to handle flasks of nuclear material to and from Hinckley Point power station. A flask of spent material is being loaded on 10th July 1997. Mineral water arrived in quantity from Inverness in 1999, to be replaced by cat food from Glasgow. (D.H.Mitchell)

95.   The results of a renovation scheme were recorded on 26th June 2002 as no. 150240 arrived from Bristol. The work on the Grade II listed structure was completed in 1994 and it included restoration of the canopies and footbridge that had been added in 1882. An old style booking office screen was restored. (M.Turvey)

BRIDGWATER DOCKS

XXV. The Bridgwater Corporation's tramway was acquired by the BER, upgraded and extended across the River Parrett to the docks, which had also been purchased along with the Bridgwater and Taunton Canal. The latter enters the non-tidal dock on the left. This map overlaps the previous one. The S & D is top right; a link line was laid in 1954 to allow the branch to be lifted but the goods yard to remain in use. It lasted until January 1967 and the entire docks branch closed in April of that year.

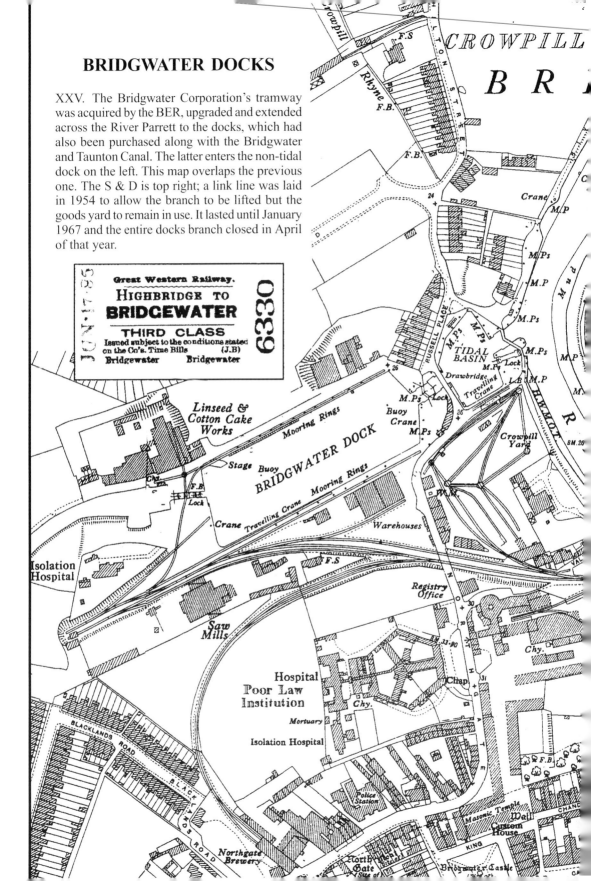

CROWPILL

B R

JUN. 1.85

Great Western Railway.

HIGHBRIDGE TO
BRIDGEWATER

THIRD CLASS

Issued subject to the conditions stated
on the Co's. Time Bills   (J.B)
Bridgewater   Bridgewater

6330

Crane
M.P
M.Ps
M.P
M.Ps
M.Ps
M.P
M.Ps
M.P

TIDAL
BASIN
Lock
Drawbridge
Travelling
Crane
L.B.
M.P
M.Ps
Lock
Crowpill
Yard
BM.26

Linseed &
Cotton Cake
Works
Mooring Rings
Buoy
Crane
M.Ps

Stage Buoy
BRIDGWATER DOCK
Mooring Rings
Crane Travelling Crane Mooring Rings
Ch.
F.B.
Lock
Warehouses

Isolation
Hospital
F.S
Registry
Office
Chy.

Saw
Mills
33.90

Hospital
Poor Law
Institution
Mortuary
Isolation Hospital
Chap
Chy.

BLACKLANDS ROAD
B L A C K L A N D S   R O A D
Northgate
Brewery
North
Gate
Site of
Police
Station
Masonic Temple
Well
Custom
House
KING
Bridgwater Castle
F.B.

G W A T E R

C a s t l e   F i e l d

Castle Field House

THE DROVE

M.P

M.Ps

Cement Lime
Brick & Tile Works

THE LEGGAR

S.B.
S.P.

S.P.

Tk

M

Cattle
Pens

Crane

Goods
Shed

W.M.

W.M.

Crane

Station

Allotment
Gardens

Crane

G.W.R.

WHARF & DOCK BRANCH

W.M.

Engine Ho.

Drawbridge

M.P

Church Street
Mills
(Corn)

Grave Yard

Vicarage Hall

P

Mud

A

R

Williams's
Buildings

L.B

St. John the Baptist's
Church
School

M.P

R

M.P

BLAKE PLACE

MONMOUTH STREET

M.Ps

M.Ps

E

Rope Walk

CHURCH STREET

F.S

T

DRY DOCK

Mud

St. John's
House

M.Ps

M.P

Saw
Mills

Crane
Water Gate
F.S.
M.Ps

QUAY

Fn.

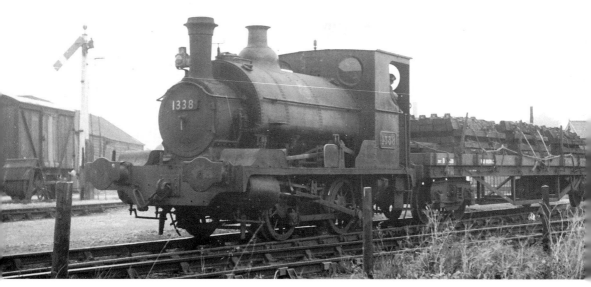

96.   No. 1338 has already been seen in picture 69 and was photographed here on 25th September 1956. There were many private sidings and coal yards on the branch. (H.C.Casserley)

97.   Crossing the drawbridge over the river on the same day was no. 1366. A stationary engine was provided to move the bridge. (H.C.Casserley)

SOUTH OF BRIDGWATER

XXVI. The BER established its carriage works south of the station and it was used for coach repairs until 1934. It is seen on the 1930 edition, by which time a commercial saw mill occupied the site of the BER foundry. The railway works was taken over by the War Department and the long traverser between the buildings remained in use until 1968. The sidings were gradually reduced so that only one remained by 2000 and that was taken out of use subsequently. Industrial activity now covers most of the area of this map.

Inset is a view of the top-hatted foreman and the traverser. (C.G.Maggs coll.)

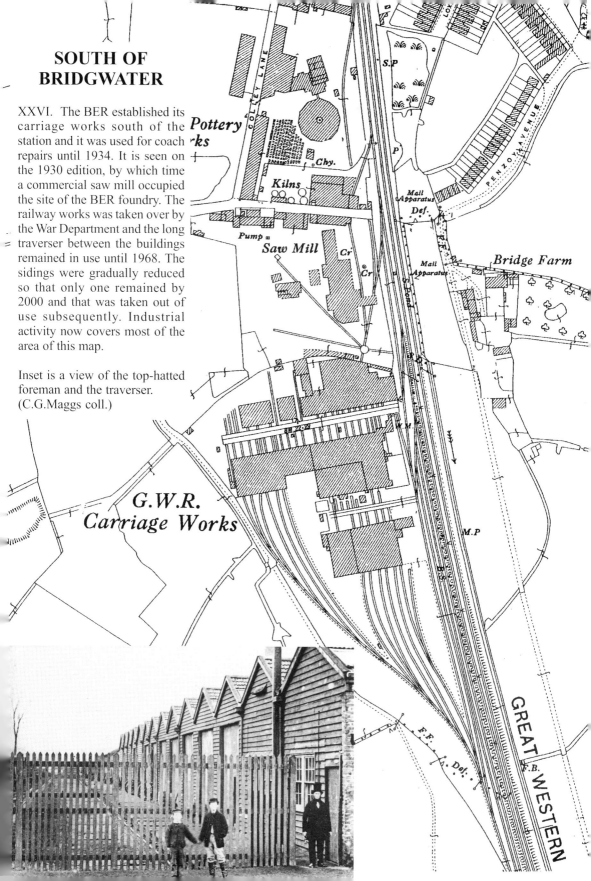

Pottery **rks**

Chy.

Kilns

Pump

Saw Mill Cr

Cr

COLLEY LANE

S.P

P

P

Mail Apparatus

Def.

Mail Apparatus

PENZOY AVENUE

Bridge Farm

G.W.R. Carriage Works

Mail Apparatus

M.P

F.F.

Def.

F.B.

GREAT WESTERN

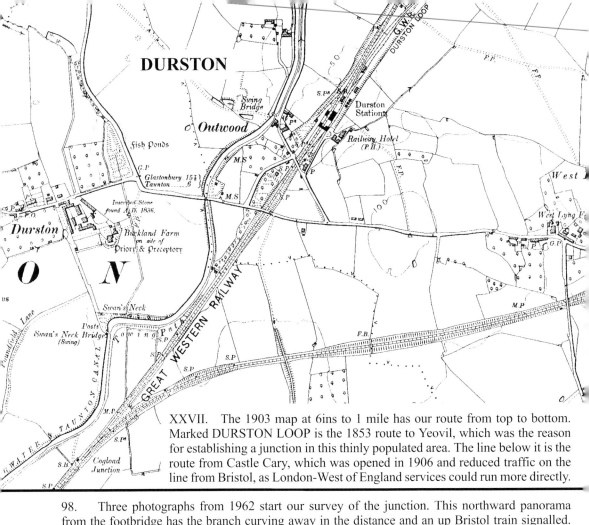

DURSTON

XXVII. The 1903 map at 6ins to 1 mile has our route from top to bottom. Marked DURSTON LOOP is the 1853 route to Yeovil, which was the reason for establishing a junction in this thinly populated area. The line below it is the route from Castle Cary, which was opened in 1906 and reduced traffic on the line from Bristol, as London-West of England services could run more directly.

98.   Three photographs from 1962 start our survey of the junction. This northward panorama from the footbridge has the branch curving away in the distance and an up Bristol train signalled. (J.H.Day)

99.   We can now enjoy two views from a train arriving from Yeovil. This includes the deserted goods shed and dock, which had earlier accommodated cattle pens. Goods service was withdrawn on 6th July 1964. (P.J.Garland/R.S.Carpenter coll.)

100.   Hand shunting using a pinch bar was seldom photographed, but often practised. The shed housed an engine and pump to raise water from a well to the tank behind.
(P.J.Garland/R.S.Carpenter coll.)

101.   Two pictures from 8th June 1963 complete our look at this then little-used junction. The fireman of no. 4143 descends to collect the single line tablet which would have been on the short post if the train had been non-stop. It is the 5.55pm all stations Taunton to Yeovil Pen Mill. (S.P.Derek)

Other views can be found in pictures 95-97 in *Westbury to Taunton* and nos 27-28 in *Branch Lines around Chard and Yeovil*.

102.   BR class 3 2-6-2T no. 82042 arrives with the 5.45pm from Yeovil and runs into the loop, which was signalled for reversible running. The 1895 71-lever signal box closed on 6th September 1965, along with the branch as far as the Castle Cary line. The station was closed to passengers on 5th October 1964, Yeovil services having been withdrawn on 15th June of that year. (S.P.Derek)

COGLOAD JUNCTION

103.   The level junction was replaced with one with a flyover for down trains from Bristol. Its progress was recorded on 13th May 1931 during the erection of 227 tons of steel. (GWR/NRM)

104.   The signal box was moved nearer Taunton and the new route opened on 15th November 1931. The 23-lever box was closed on 7th April 1986. (P.J.Garland/R.S.Carpenter coll.)

105.   The skew structure was photographed on 28th February 1977 with nos 47478 and 47105 working the 08.20 Birmingham to Plymouth. (T.Heavyside)

106.   An atmospheric shot from 26th November 1984 shows the incline over the flyover and part of the once railway owned Bridgwater & Taunton Canal. No. 50019 *Ramillies* is hauling the 07.30 Penzance to Aberdeen. (G.Gillham)

CREECH ST. MICHAEL HALT

107.   The River Tone flooded the track in 1894 and a 2201 class 2-4-0 was photographed with an up train at the site of the future halt. (R.S.Carpenter coll.)

108.   Water on the tracks was well controlled when water troughs were installed. No. 5422 was working a stopping service to Castle Cary in August 1955. Trains running via Durston were the only ones that could call at the halt. (P.J.Garland/R.S.Carpenter coll.)

109.   The halt opened on 13th August 1928, but had to be completely rebuilt in 1931 during the quadrupling. This eastward view is from August 1962 and includes one of a pair of brick-built buildings, unusually substantial for a halt. (P.J.Garland/R.S.Carpenter coll.)

110.   A westward panorama features Creech Paper Mills, the other side of which there was a siding from the Chard branch. This lost its passenger service in 1962, but the siding remained until 1966. The halt closed on 5th October 1964 and the outer tracks were not used after 1986. (Lens of Sutton)

111.   The GWR Concrete Works produced a vast variety of components for signalling, track, drains, lighting and structural purposes. It started in a small way in about 1899 and declined in the 1980s, the site being developed for housing. The works was extended onto a seven acre area in 1912. (GWR/NRM)

112.   The Eastern Link Road was fairly new when this photograph was taken from it on 26th November 1984. No. 50021 *Rodney* is heading the 09.36 Liverpool to Penzance on the down relief line, which was taken out of use on 9th May 1986. (G.Gillham)

113. A view from the other side of the road on 12th August 1983 features no. 50049 *Defiance* with the 11.38 Plymouth to Manchester service. The goods lines (left) avoided the station and ran to the south of it and East Junction Box. This had 147 levers and a panel was added on 12th May 1986, at which time the goods lines were disconnected. The box closed on 23rd March 1987. The former signal works is in the centre background (G.Gillham)

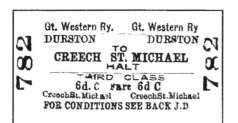

Gt. Western Ry.   Gt. Western Ry
DURSTON   DURSTON
782   TO   782
CREECH ST. MICHAEL
HALT
THIRD CLASS
6d. C   fare   6d C
CreechSt.Michael   CreechSt.Michael
FOR CONDITIONS SEE BACK J.D

Gt. Western Ry   Gt Western Ry
H.M. FORCES ON LEAVE
Creech St. Michael   Creech St. Michael
644   HALT   HALT   644
TO
TAUNTON
THIRD CLASS
Taunton   Taunton
FOR CONDITIONS SEE BACK   W.H

TAUNTON

114.   No. 4924 *Eydon Hall* arrives with an up express on 13th September 1958. The station had two locomotives specifically for shunting at this time. (N.L.Browne)

115.   Class 9F 2-10-0 no. 92240 departs with an up express on 1st August 1959 and will soon pass East Junction Box. The short siding in the foreground could be used for changing engines and has a pit. (P.J.Kelley)

116.   The London end of the station was recorded on a dull day in December 1963. The bay platform on the left was often used by Chard trains. (C.L.Caddy)

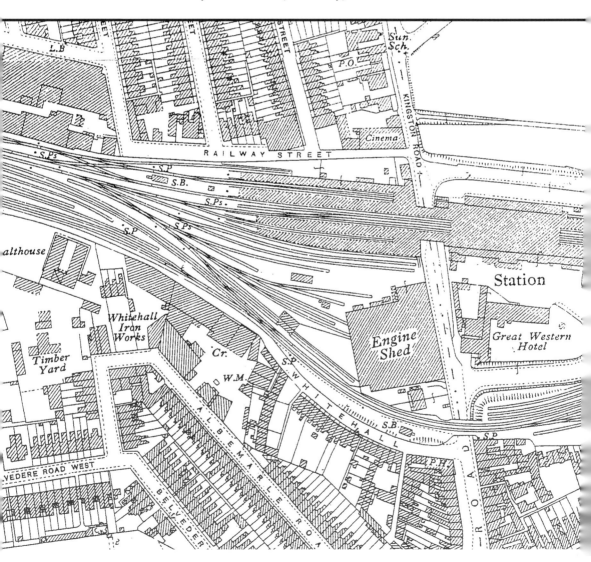

WELLESLEY STREET

Allotment Gardens

XXVIII. The first station had both platforms on the southern track, but this was rebuilt in 1868 with a roof across the lines, as shown on this 1929 map. Bay platforms were created in 1895. Part of the route of the 1896 goods lines south of the engine shed was on the alignment of the canal, which, subsequent to its closure westwards, ended at Firepool Lock, lower right. The overall roof was lost during major alterations to provide four tracks through the station in 1931.

WOOD ROAD

MALVERN TERRACE

MALVERN TERRACE

Cement Works

P.H.

F.P.

Engineering Works

W.M.

S.P.   M.P.

S.B.

S.P.

S.P.

62

S.P.

W.M.

N.P.

S.B.

S.Ps

.Cr   GREAT WESTERN RAILWAY

Pumping Station

Goods Shed

W.M.

Reservoir

51

ROAD

FIREPOOL

St.   Firepool Lock

F.B.   Firepool Weir

St.

N A I L

Allotm

117.   The station was extended northwards during its expansion in 1931 and this new entrance was provided. The rear of the refreshment and waiting rooms are in this view from about 1976. (P.J.Kelley)

118.   The island platform (left) was closed on 6th March 1967 only to be brought back into use in May 2000. No. 46009 is taking empty china clay wagons back to Cornwall on 16th May 1979. After 1986, signalling was undertaken from a panel at Exeter and these two lines were signalled for reversible running. (T.Heavyside)

119.   We finish our visit to this busy station with two photographs from 28th March 2001. This one was taken from the reopened and resurfaced platform 4 and features a class 158 "Super Sprinter" bound for Bristol. (M.Turvey)

120.   Almost new, no. 67027 heads an up mail train through platform 5 and passes the remains of the GWR signal works. The platforms had been renumbered in 1986 and again in 2000; bay no. 6 is obscured by the train. From it we could take a stopping train back to Bristol and enjoy the journey over again. (M.Turvey)

Taunton is also featured in the following albums:
Branch Lines to Chard and Yeovil
Branch Line to Minehead
Exeter and Taunton Tramways
Taunton to Exeter
Westbury to Taunton
Taunton to Barnstaple

Middleton Press

Easebourne Lane, Midhurst, W Sussex. GU29 9AZ Tel: 01730 813169 Fax: 01730 812601
Email: enquiries@middletonpress.fsnet.co.uk *If books are not available from your
local transport stockist, order direct with cheque, Visa or Mastercard, post free UK.*

BRANCH LINES
Branch Line to Allhallows
Branch Line to Alton
Branch Lines around Ascot
Branch Line to Ashburton
Branch Lines around Bodmin
Branch Line to Bude
Branch Lines around Canterbury
Branch Lines around Chard & Yeovil
Branch Line to Cheddar
Branch Lines around Cromer
Branch Lines to East Grinstead
Branch Lines of East London
Branch Lines to Effingham Junction
Branch Lines around Exmouth
Branch Lines to Falmouth, Helston & St. Ives
Branch Line to Fairford
Branch Lines around Gosport
Branch Line to Hayling
Branch Lines to Henley, Windsor & Marlow
Branch Line to Hawkhurst
Branch Lines around Huntingdon
Branch Line to Ilfracombe
Branch Line to Kingsbridge
Branch Line to Kingswear
Branch Line to Lambourn
Branch Lines to Launceston & Princetown
Branch Lines to Longmoor
Branch Line to Looe
Branch Line to Lyme Regis
Branch Lines around Midhurst
Branch Line to Minehead
Branch Line to Moretonhampstead
Branch Lines to Newport (IOW)
Branch Lines to Newquay
Branch Lines around North Woolwich
Branch Line to Padstow
Branch Lines around Plymouth
Branch Lines to Princes Risborough
Branch Lines to Seaton and Sidmouth
Branch Lines around Sheerness
Branch Line to Shrewsbury
Branch Line to Swanage *updated*
Branch Line to Tenterden
Branch Lines around Tiverton
Branch Lines to Torrington
Branch Line to Upwell
Branch Lines of West London
Branch Lines around Weymouth
Branch Lines around Wimborne
Branch Lines around Wisbech

NARROW GAUGE
Branch Line to Lynton
Branch Lines around Portmadoc 1923-46
Branch Lines around Porthmadog 1954-94
Branch Line to Southwold
Douglas to Port Erin
Douglas to Peel
Kent Narrow Gauge
Northern France Narrow Gauge
Romneyrail
Southern France Narrow Gauge
Sussex Narrow Gauge
Surrey Narrow Gauge
Swiss Narrow Gauge
Two-Foot Gauge Survivors
Vivarais Narrow Gauge

SOUTH COAST RAILWAYS
Ashford to Dover
Bournemouth to Weymouth
Brighton to Worthing
Eastbourne to Hastings
Hastings to Ashford
Portsmouth to Southampton
Ryde to Ventnor
Southampton to Bournemouth

SOUTHERN MAIN LINES
Basingstoke to Salisbury
Bromley South to Rochester
Crawley to Littlehampton
Dartford to Sittingbourne
East Croydon to Three Bridges
Epsom to Horsham
Exeter to Barnstaple
Exeter to Tavistock
Faversham to Dover
London Bridge to East Croydon
Orpington to Tonbridge
Tonbridge to Hastings
Salisbury to Yeovil
Sittingbourne to Ramsgate
Swanley to Ashford
Tavistock to Plymouth
Three Bridges to Brighton
Victoria to Bromley South
Victoria to East Croydon
Waterloo to Windsor
Waterloo to Woking
Woking to Portsmouth
Woking to Southampton
Yeovil to Exeter

EASTERN MAIN LINES
Barking to Southend
Ely to Kings Lynn
Ely to Norwich
Fenchurch Street to Barking
Ilford to Shenfield
Ipswich to Saxmundham
Liverpool Street to Ilford
Saxmundham to Yarmouth
Tilbury Loop

WESTERN MAIN LINES
Bristol to Taunton
Didcot to Banbury
Didcot to Swindon
Ealing to Slough
Exeter to Newton Abbot
Newton Abbot to Plymouth
Newbury to Westbury
Paddington to Ealing
Paddington to Princes Risborough
Plymouth to St. Austell
Princes Risborough to Banbury
Reading to Didcot
Slough to Newbury
St. Austell to Penzance
Swindon to Bristol
Taunton to Exeter
Westbury to Taunton

MIDLAND MAIN LINES
Euston to Harrow & Wealdstone
St. Pancras to St. Albans

COUNTRY RAILWAY ROUTES
Abergavenny to Merthyr
Andover to Southampton
Bath to Evercreech Junction
Bath Green Park to Bristol
Burnham to Evercreech Junction
Cheltenham to Andover
Croydon to East Grinstead
Didcot to Winchester
East Kent Light Railway
Fareham to Salisbury
Guildford to Redhill
Reading to Basingstoke
Reading to Guildford
Redhill to Ashford
Salisbury to Westbury
Stratford upon Avon to Cheltenham
Strood to Paddock Wood
Taunton to Barnstaple
Wenford Bridge to Fowey
Westbury to Bath
Woking to Alton
Yeovil to Dorchester

GREAT RAILWAY ERAS
Ashford from Steam to Eurostar
Clapham Junction 50 years of change
Festiniog in the Fifties
Festiniog in the Sixties
Festiniog 50 years of enterprise
Isle of Wight Lines 50 years of change
Railways to Victory 1944-46
Return to Blaenau 1970-82
SECR Centenary album
Talyllyn 50 years of change
Yeovil 50 years of change

LONDON SUBURBAN RAILWAYS
Caterham and Tattenham Corner
Charing Cross to Dartford
Clapham Jn. to Beckenham Jn.
Crystal Palace (HL) & Catford Loop
East London Line
Finsbury Park to Alexandra Palace
Holbourn Viaduct to Lewisham
Kingston and Hounslow Loops
Lewisham to Dartford
Lines around Wimbledon
Liverpool Street to Chingford
London Bridge to Addiscombe
Mitcham Junction Lines
North London Line
South London Line
West Croydon to Epsom
West London Line
Willesden Junction to Richmond
Wimbledon to Beckenham
Wimbledon to Epsom

STEAMING THROUGH
Steaming through Cornwall
Steaming through the Isle of Wight
Steaming through Kent
Steaming through West Hants

TRAMWAY CLASSICS
Aldgate & Stepney Tramways
Barnet & Finchley Tramways
Bath Tramways
Brighton's Tramways
Bristol's Tramways
Burton & Ashby Tramways
Camberwell & W.Norwood Tramways
Clapham & Streatham Tramways
Croydon's Tramways
Dover's Tramways
East Ham & West Ham Tramways
Edgware and Willesden Tramways
Eltham & Woolwich Tramways
Embankment & Waterloo Tramways
Enfield & Wood Green Tramways
Exeter & Taunton Tramways
Greenwich & Dartford Tramways
Hammersmith & Hounslow Tramways
Hampstead & Highgate Tramways
Hastings Tramways
Holborn & Finsbury Tramways
Ilford & Barking Tramways
Kingston & Wimbledon Tramways
Lewisham & Catford Tramways
Liverpool Tramways 1. Eastern Routes
Liverpool Tramways 2. Southern Routes
Liverpool Tramways 3. Northern Routes
Maidstone & Chatham Tramways
Margate to Ramsgate
North Kent Tramways
Norwich Tramways
Reading Tramways
Seaton & Eastbourne Tramways
Shepherds Bush & Uxbridge Tramways
Southend-on-sea Tramways
Southwark & Deptford Tramways
Stamford Hill Tramways
Twickenham & Kingston Tramways
Victoria & Lambeth Tramways
Waltham Cross & Edmonton Tramways
Walthamstow & Leyton Tramways
Wandsworth & Battersea Tramways

TROLLEYBUS CLASSICS
Croydon Trolleybuses
Derby Trolleybuses
Hastings Trolleybuses
Huddersfield Trolleybuses
Maidstone Trolleybuses
Portsmouth Trolleybuses
Woolwich & Dartford Trolleybuses

WATERWAY ALBUMS
Kent and East Sussex Waterways
London to Portsmouth Waterway
West Sussex Waterways

MILITARY BOOKS
Battle over Portsmouth
Battle over Sussex 1940
Bombers over Sussex 1943-45
Bognor at War
Military Defence of West Sussex
Military Signals from the South Coast
Secret Sussex Resistance
Surrey Home Guard

OTHER RAILWAY BOOKS
Index to all Middleton Press stations
Industrial Railways of the South-East
South Eastern & Chatham Railways
London Chatham & Dover Railway
London Termini - Past and Proposed
War on the Line (SR 1939-45)

BIOGRAPHY
Garraway Father & Son